DISASTER!
IN NATURE

Jen Green

Belitha Press

LOOK FOR THE VOLCANO

Look for the volcano in boxes like this.
Here you will find extra facts, stories and other
interesting information about disasters in nature.

Produced by
Roger Coote Publishing
Gissing's Farm, Fressingfield
Suffolk IP21 5SH, UK

First published in the UK in 2002 by
Belitha Press
A member of Chrysalis Books plc
64 Brewery Road, London N7 9NT

Designer: Victoria Webb
Editor: Kate Phelps
Picture Research: Lynda Lines

ISBN 1 84138 409 7

British Library Cataloguing in Publication Data for this
book is available from the British Library.

Printed in Taiwan
10 9 8 7 6 5 4 3 2 1

Acknowledgements
We wish to thank the following individuals and
organizations for their help and assistance and for
supplying material in their collections: AKG back cover
top, 18, 23 top; Associated Press back cover bottom left
(Katsumi Kasahara), 5 bottom (Zaheeruddin
Abdullah), 15 (Katsumi Kasahara); Bruce Coleman
Collection front cover (Pacific Stock), 17 top (Astrofoto);
Corbis 1 (Nik Wheeler), 3 (Peter Turnley), 4 top (Roger
Ressmeyer), 6 (Peter Turnley), 7 top (Tom Bean), 8
(Lloyd Cluff), 9 top (Owen Franken), 14 (Bettmann), 19
bottom (Bettmann), 20 (Bettmann), 22 (Bradley Smith),
23 bottom, 24 (Nik Wheeler), 25 bottom (Peter Turnley),
28 (Lloyd Cluff), 31 (Roger Ressmeyer); Corbis Digital
Stock 10 top, 29; FLPA 5 top (Larry West), 11 bottom (J
Lynch), 12 top (S Jonasson), 19 top (Derek Middleton),
21 bottom (SC Brown), 26 bottom (Steve McCutcheon),
27 top (Panda Photo); MPM Images 27 bottom (Daniel
Rogers); Rex Features 2, 12 bottom, 13, 25 top; Topham
Picturepoint back cover bottom right, 7 bottom, 11 top,
21 top. Artwork on pages 4 and 10 by Peter Bull. Artwork
on pages 16-17 and 30 by Michael Posen. Artwork on
page 26 by Tony Townsend.

*◄A cloud of ash races down
a mountainside in Japan as a
volcano erupts.*

CONTENTS

► *Survivors of an earthquake in Armenia sit among their ruined homes.*

DEADLY PLANET

Planet Earth often acts like a kind mother to us. It provides rich soil for plants to grow and water for us to drink. But our planet seems to turn against us when earthquakes hit and volcanoes erupt.

▲ A river of red-hot, melted rock surges down a mountain in Italy as a volcano erupts.

The ground under our feet seems cold and solid, but it is not like that all the way through. Far underground, the rocks that form our planet are so hot they melt. Deep inside the Earth are amazingly powerful natural forces. They break loose when volcanoes erupt and earthquakes strike.

INSIDE THE EARTH

Planet Earth is not solid all the way through, but is made up of three main layers. At the very centre is the super-hot core. Beneath the surface crust is the mantle, a layer of red-hot rock which is soft and squishy. Hot, liquid rock from the mantle surges up to the surface when a volcano erupts.

◀ This diagram shows the main layers found inside the Earth. The core is the hottest part of all.

Outer core

Inner core

Mantle

Crust

Insects called mosquitoes, shown here, spread a deadly disease called malaria.

Earthquakes and eruptions sometimes do terrible damage to a huge area. Villages, towns and even whole cities may be destroyed. Landslides, avalanches, floods, fires and giant ocean waves may follow, causing even more damage. Hundreds, even thousands, of people and animals may die.

Everyday life on Earth is also threatened by other natural hazards. In country areas, hundreds of people may go hungry if their crops are attacked by an animal plague. Thousands may die if a disease breaks out that doctors can find no cure for. This book looks at just some of the natural dangers faced by people around the world.

This village in Afghanistan in Asia has been wrecked by an earthquake.

SHAKING EARTH

Earthquakes are the most terrifying and destructive of all natural forces. In just seconds, they can shatter whole towns and kill thousands of people.

▼ *The Armenian earthquake destroyed these people's homes.*

On 7 December 1988, the republic of Armenia in central Asia was hit by a massive earthquake. Just before midday, the people of Leninakan, Armenia's second-largest city, heard a terrible rumbling sound, like an express train racing past.

WHY EARTHQUAKES HAPPEN

Earth's outer crust is made up of giant sections called plates that fit together like pieces in an enormous jigsaw. The plates drift like rafts on the red-hot, liquid layer below. As two plates move against one another, they may stick for a time, then suddenly jolt into a new position. It is the jolt that causes a quake.

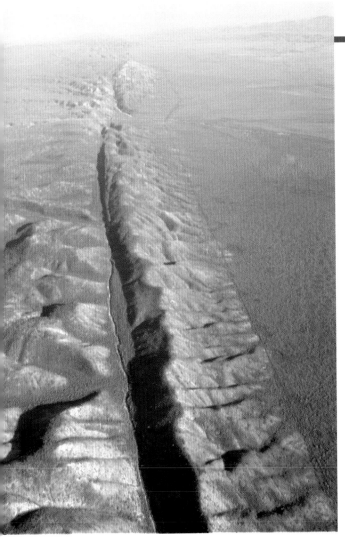

As the earthquake struck, the ground trembled and shook violently. Pavements shattered as the ground underneath was ripped apart. Buildings rocked like ships in a rough sea, then toppled over. Jets of steam burst from the ground. Everyone was terrified.

Just minutes later, two-thirds of Leninakan lay in ruins. Many small towns and villages in the region were simply wiped out. Altogether, nearly 30 000 people died in the earthquake. It was the worst to strike the region in nearly a century. It took Armenia many years to recover from the quake.

▲ *The area where two plates meet and rub together is called a faultline. From above, the faultine looks like a giant crack in the Earth. Earthquakes often strike along faultlines like this one in the western USA.*

▼ *The city of San Franscisco in the USA lies near a faultline. A terrible earthquake struck the city in 1906, as shown in this picture. Another quake struck in 1989.*

AFTER THE QUAKE

Even the most powerful earthquake lasts only a few minutes. But landslides, avalanches, fires and other dangers may follow after the quake.

A religious statue stands on Cemetery Hill above Yungay, where people fled to escape the 1970 quake.

On 31 May 1970, a powerful earthquake struck Peru in South America. It destroyed homes in towns and villages over a wide area high in the Andes Mountains. But the town of Yungay, in a valley below the mountains, was the most badly hit.

Yungay lay below a snow-covered peak called Mount Huascarán. When the earthquake struck, a large chunk of snow and rock broke off the mountain and swept downhill in an avalanche. As the avalanche gathered speed, huge boulders were dragged along with it. Yungay was right in its path.

ON SHAKY GROUND

An unusual thing can happen when an earthquake strikes an area where the soil is made of sand or gravel. The quake may cause the ground to become soft. Buildings may become unsteady and fall over. This effect caused great destruction in Mexico City during the 1985 quake.

By chance, the earthquake struck during the 1970 World Cup football competition. In Yungay most people were indoors, watching a match. As the earth shook, they rushed outside to see a huge wall of rocks, ice and mud surging towards them. A few people managed to scramble uphill to a cemetery, but most of Yungay's 20 000 inhabitants were buried alive or swept away.

▶ *In 1985, a major earthquake struck Mexico City, one of the world's largest cities. Thousands of buildings were damaged when the soft soil of the city collapsed.*

◄ *A volcano on an island in Hawaii in the Pacific Ocean shoots red-hot lava high into the air.*

THE FURY OF VOLCANOES

Hot, melted rock from deep underground spurts through a hole in the Earth's crust when a volcano erupts. Giant clouds of ash, gas, steam and fiery sparks shoot high into the air.

Nearly 2000 years ago, a Roman writer called Pliny the Younger watched the eruption of Mount Vesuvius in southern Italy. He lived near Pompeii, a town below the peak. The volcano had been quiet for 800 years. Then, in AD 79, it suddenly erupted.

WHAT HAPPENS WHEN A VOLCANO ERUPTS?

Red-hot, melted rock surges up from underground in the weeks before a volcano erupts. It collects in a hollow chamber under the volcano. The pressure builds up and up, until finally, the volcano explodes. Rocks and ash soar into the air. Melted rock called lava spurts from the crater (opening). Layers of ash and lava build up to make a mountain.

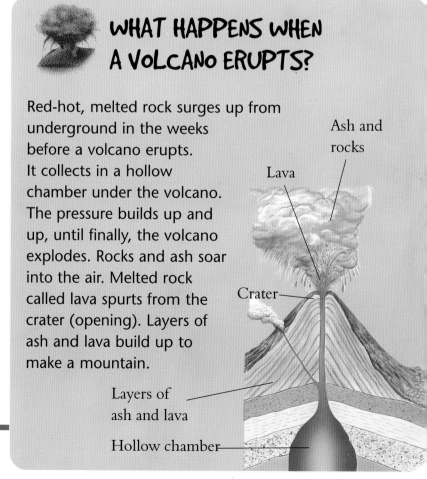

Ash and rocks

Lava

Crater

Layers of ash and lava

Hollow chamber

Pompeii lay buried under a thick layer of ash for centuries, but in the eighteenth century it was uncovered. The bodies of the dead citizens left hollows in the hardened ash, from which plaster casts could be made. This is a cast of a Roman man.

A tall, black cloud of smoke shaped like a pine tree rose high in the air. Burning, poisonous gas swept down the mountainside and into Pompeii. The townspeople burned or choked to death in the fumes.

From the nearby port of Misenum, Pliny watched the eruption with his mother and his uncle. Pliny's uncle set off by boat to take a closer look, and was never seen again. Pliny and his mother fled to the hills as smoke spread towards them. They ran as ash and stones rained down. Later, they returned home to find a thick layer of ash covering the countryside.

In 1980, a volcano called Mount St Helens in the western USA erupted without warning. The whole top blew off the mountain. Tonnes of ash and rock spilled down the mountainsides, causing landslides and flattening nearby forests.

IN THE VOLCANO'S PATH

Tonnes of glowing lava ooze down the mountain when a volcano erupts. Burning ash may mix with snow or water to form a swift-moving flow called a lahar. It roars downhill at high speed and destroys anything in its path.

▶ *Lava sets homes on fire in Iceland.*

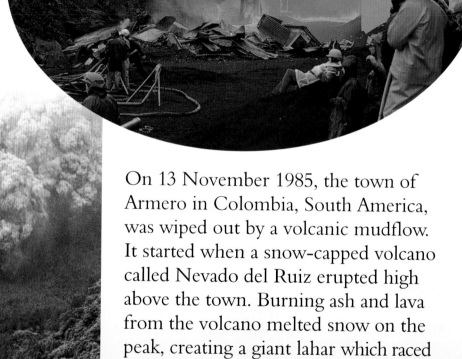

On 13 November 1985, the town of Armero in Colombia, South America, was wiped out by a volcanic mudflow. It started when a snow-capped volcano called Nevado del Ruiz erupted high above the town. Burning ash and lava from the volcano melted snow on the peak, creating a giant lahar which raced downhill at about 150 km/h.

◀ *When Mount Fugen in Japan erupted in 1991, 'glowing clouds' of burning ash and steam raced downhill at over 100 km/h. Thirty-eight people died. They included some volcano experts who had come to survey the scene.*

▲ Houses in Armero lie buried by the tide of ash and mud that swept down from the mountain in 1985.

VOLCANOES AT SEA

Some eruptions happen at sea. If the volcano goes on erupting, so much lava eventually builds up that the mound rises above the sea to make an island. In 1963, sailors fishing off the coast of Iceland saw a tall cloud of smoke rising from the sea. The next day, the volcano broke the surface. The new island was named Surtsey, after the Icelandic god of fire.

A 16-year-old girl called Slaye Molina was at home in Armero when the tide of mud struck. Slaye reported: 'People screamed, "The world is ending!" We rushed outside.' The safest place to be was on high ground. Slaye and others raced uphill. Some people climbed on top of their houses and clung on as the tide swept past.

Slaye was one of the lucky few who survived the disaster. Over 23 000 people died as the mud sucked them down like quicksand or buried them alive. She spent three days on the hilltop until it was safe to come down.

WALLS OF WATER

When earthquakes strike or volcanoes erupt at sea, they can cause huge waves of water, called tsunamis, to race across the ocean. These waves cause great destruction when they reach land.

▲ *In 1755, Lisbon was wrecked by three different natural forces. The earthquake brought buildings tumbling down. The harbour was swamped by giant waves. Candles in ruined churches also started fires. Altogether, 50 000 people died.*

On 1 November 1755, the port of Lisbon in Portugal was wrecked by tsunamis. They were caused when an earthquake shook the seabed off the coast. Lisbon was a thriving port with beautiful churches. It was a holy day, and most people were in church.

Suddenly the city was shaken by a violent earthquake. An eyewitness saw buildings swaying backwards and forwards 'like a wheat field blowing in a breeze'. In the harbour, astonished sailors watched all the water drain away suddenly. Boats and fish were stranded. Moments later, a giant wall of water appeared and rushed towards the town.

As the wave struck, boats were flung on to the quayside. Buildings collapsed as the water crashed down. People and animals were sucked into the sea as the wave retreated. Hundreds of people drowned.

▼ *In 1993, this Japanese port was wrecked by a tsunami started by an undersea earthquake. The giant wave overturned boats and cars on the quay.*

IN DEEP WATER

Tsunamis cause low but very powerful waves out in the deep ocean. The waves only rear up to form huge crests as they reach shallow water near land. In 1896, the Japanese island of Honshu was hit by tsunamis that destroyed many coastal towns and killed 28 000 people. Fishermen working out to sea did not even notice the waves as they slipped under their boats.

MISSILES FROM SPACE

The planet we live on is also menaced by natural forces from outer space – deadly missiles called meteorites. These great chunks of rock fall from the skies to crash on to Earth's surface. The biggest leave huge, hollow craters on the ground.

In the distant past, 65 million years ago, the dinosaurs and many other animals all died out suddenly. Some scientists believe that these extinctions may have been caused by a giant meteorite.

SHOOTING STARS

Millions of meteors fall to Earth from space each year, but most are tiny. They burn up as they enter our planet's atmosphere, leaving fiery trails across the sky. We call these bright streaks shooting stars. Only the very largest survive the trip to land on Earth.

◄ Barringer's Crater in Arizona, USA, is a deep hollow left by a meteorite that crashed to Earth thousands of years ago. The crater is 180m deep and 1.2 km wide – large enough to swallow a whole village.

The crashing meteorite may have raised a huge cloud of dust that blotted out the sun for years. Without sunlight, plants withered and died, so there was no food for the dinosaurs to eat.

Not all scientists agree with this theory. Some experts believe that the dinosaurs died after a massive volcanic eruption. The eruption sent huge clouds of ash into the air, which again blotted out the sunlight. Earth's weather changed rapidly and became much, much colder. The dinosaurs could not cope with the sudden cold, so they died out.

▼ At various times in Earth's history, huge meteorites have crashed to the ground, leaving giant craters. Did an enormous meteorite cause the dinosaurs to die out 65 million years ago?

KILLER DISEASES

At various times in history, thousands of people have died from large-scale outbreaks of disease called plagues or epidemics.

In the fourteenth century, a plague called the Black Death swept across Europe and Asia. Millions died. It was a form of a disease we call bubonic plague. The Black Death was the worst plague in history. Experts guess it killed up to 25 million people – a third of all the people in Europe and Asia.

▲ *The Black Death killed so many people in Europe that whole villages were deserted. This fourteenth-century illustration shows people burying the dead.*

Plague victims soon became sick, giddy and feverish. Later, dark patches and swellings appeared on their bodies. Death followed in a few days.

The Black Death raged for seven years, and then died out naturally. Since the fourteenth century, there have been several more outbreaks of the killer disease, but none has been as bad.

▶ *The plague was spread by rats that carried fleas infected with the deadly illness. When the fleas hopped on to people and bit them, they caught the disease.*

◀ *In 1918, people wore masks to try to stop the deadly 'flu from spreading. In some cities, you could be arrested for coughing or sneezing!*

KILLER 'FLU

In 1918, an outbreak of influenza ('flu) swept around the world just as the First World War was ending. It killed a total of 21 million people – far more than had died in the war.

BLIGHT AND ANIMAL PLAGUES

Some natural disasters are caused by plagues of insects or other animals, or even by tiny fungi (like miniature mushrooms). Some fungi produce a disease called blight which can destroy whole harvests. When this happens, local people starve.

▼ *This painting shows Irish people arriving in Canada in the 1840s. They fled their homeland to start a new life after blight destroyed the potato crops.*

A NEW LIFE

Following the famine of the 1840s, millions of Irish people left to start a new life in the United States and Canada. The immigrants (people arriving) included the ancestors of US president John F Kennedy and Henry Ford, who founded the Ford car company. Altogether, Ireland lost a third of all its people through starvation and emigration (people leaving).

In Ireland in the 1840s, a blight attacked the potato harvest. Ireland had several years of very wet weather. The blight thrived in the damp conditions. Year after year, the potato crop failed. Potatoes were the main source of food for Irish country people. The blight turned the precious potato crops black and rotten. With no food to eat, about a million people starved to death.

Throughout history, plagues of animals have also caused widespread hardship and starvation. In Africa, huge swarms of insects called locusts sometimes descend on crops and quickly eat whole fields bare.

▶ *The Bible's Old Testament records that a plague of locusts struck ancient Egypt 3500 years ago.*

▼ *A huge swarm of locusts darkens the sky above a marsh in southern Africa.*

AMAZING ESCAPES

Earthquakes, volcanoes, plagues and other natural disasters can kill thousands of people. Sometimes, just a few people have a lucky escape.

In 1902, a volcano called Mount Pelée on the island of Martinique in the Caribbean erupted. The bustling port of St Pierre lay just below the peak. Sailors on ships in the bay heard the noise of a massive explosion, like a thousand cannons going off at once. They looked up as a sheet of flame swept down the mountain and a cloud of black smoke swallowed the town.

▲ *A boy stands by the ruined prison cell in which Ludger Sylbaris survived the blast from Mount Pelée.*

YOUNG SURVIVOR

The 1985 earthquake that hit Mexico City shattered many buildings in the city centre. The main hospital collapsed floor by floor, and 600 patients and medical staff inside were killed. After two days, rescuers found a very young survivor among the heaps of rubble. It was a baby who had been born just minutes before the earthquake struck.

The blast and the cloud of burning, poisonous gas killed 38 000 people in St Pierre in just a few minutes. One of the very few survivors was a man called Ludger Sylbaris, who had been imprisoned in the local jail.

◀ When Mount Vesuvius erupted in AD 79, Pliny and his mother were lucky to survive the blast.

The thick walls of the prison protected Sylbaris from the blast. He later reported hearing a huge noise, and then people calling for help. 'Everyone cried out "I am burning! I am dying!" Five minutes later, there were no more cries except mine.' After three days, rescuers found Sylbaris in the wreckage of the prison. He was burned, terrified and thirsty, but he survived.

▼ This old photo shows the scene after St Pierre was hit by the volcanic explosion. Many buildings were completely flattened by the blast. A ravine channelled the cloud of burning gases straight into the town.

RACING TO THE RESCUE

When disaster strikes, rescue teams arrive on the scene as quickly as possible. They race against time to try to save as many people as they can.

Just getting to the scene of a natural disaster is often difficult. Roads, bridges and railways are often shattered. Often the only way to reach the stricken area is by plane. At the disaster, medical teams and equipment will be urgently needed. Earth-moving equipment, from spades to bulldozers, will help to shift the piles of rubble. Generators will provide power if there is no electricity. Most of these vital supplies arrive by air.

 **WISE ADVICE**

After the Lisbon earthquake of 1755, the king of Portugal asked a trusted counsellor for advice on how to deal with the disaster. The nobleman replied: 'Sire, we must bury the dead and feed the living.' This advice still holds true in many areas struck by natural disasters in modern times.

▲ *In 1985, rescue workers in Mexico City used a crane to help clear the rubble as they searched for survivors.*

◀A rescue worker tries to free a boy trapped in a ruined building in Armero after the mudflow struck in 1985.

Once on the scene, rescue teams check the damage and try to find survivors as quickly as possible. Trained sniffer dogs may help to find people buried in ruined buildings. Or rescuers may use heat-sensing cameras that can pick up people's body heat. Medical staff give injured people emergency treatment. The worst cases are usually rushed to hospital. Other survivors are given food, blankets and shelter.

Many countries often join in the rescue effort. After the earthquake disaster in Armenia, medical teams, equipment, food and shelter were sent by countries around the world.

▶Helpers rush an injured man to hospital following the Armenian earthquake.

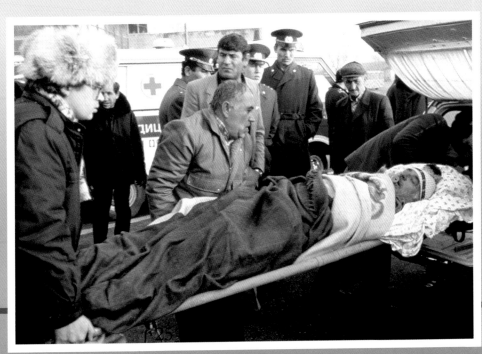

DISASTER FACTS

WORST QUAKES

The deadliest earthquake in history struck the Shanx region of China in 1556. Around 830 000 people were killed. The worst quake of modern times also happened in China, this time in Tangshan province in 1976. Around 240 000 people are thought to have died in the disaster.

SINKING FEELING

In 1964, Alaska was rocked by one of North America's worst earthquakes. Tidal waves caused by the quake destroyed the port of Valdez. In some regions, the quake turned solid ground soft and buildings sank into the mud.

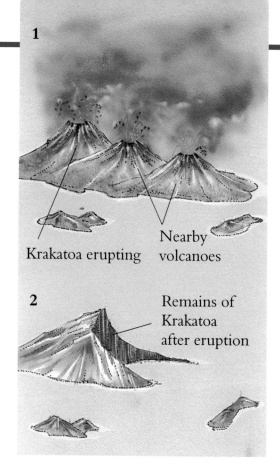

The huge eruption of Mount Krakatoa in 1883 destroyed several other volcanic islands nearby.

THE BIG ONE

The 1815 eruption of Mount Tambora, on the island of Sumbawa in Indonesia, was the largest ever recorded. It killed around 90 000 people and caused great destruction. The erupting volcano threw an estimated 80 cubic km of ash into the air. The dust cloud spread right round the world. It blotted out the sunlight and caused temperatures to fall.

Buildings sink into the soft soil after the Alaskan earthquake of 1964.

THE LOUDEST BANG

The 1883 eruption of Mount Krakatoa in Indonesia caused the biggest explosion in history. The bang was heard on islands more than 4500 km from the blast.

Mount Krakatoa is still erupting.

GIANT VOLCANO

The world's largest volcano is Mauna Loa on the island of Hawaii. It rises to a height of 4170m and measures 120 km long and 50 km wide. Mauna Loa is a very active volcano. On average, it erupts once every 4.5 years.

THE LEGEND OF ATLANTIS

The Greek legend of the lost city of Atlantis describes a beautiful city which sank beneath the waves after a mysterious disaster. Experts believe the story may have been inspired by a real disaster that happened in ancient times. Around 1470 BC, the volcanic island of Santorini in the Aegean Sea off Greece exploded in a huge eruption. Tidal waves spread across the ocean and swamped towns on nearby islands, including Crete.

ONE IN 50 MILLION

In 1908, a huge meteorite exploded 8 km above Siberia in Russia. The explosion sent shock waves around the world but surprisingly, left no crater. Experts calculate that a meteorite of this size only crashes through Earth's atmosphere once every 50 million years.

The Transamerica Building in San Francisco, USA, is designed to survive an earthquake.

DISASTER WORDS

Black Death A major outbreak of a disease called the bubonic plague that swept across Europe and Asia in the fourteenth century. The Black Death killed millions of people. It was the worst plague in recorded history.

Blight A plant disease which may be caused by a fungus (a type of mushroom).

Core The super-hot centre of the Earth.

Crater An opening at the top of a volcano through which lava, gas, ash and steam surge during an eruption.

Crust The outer layer of Earth's surface.

Emigrate To leave one's own country and move to a different one.

Epidemic A widespread outbreak of a disease such as the bubonic plague.

Erupt When a volcano explodes.

Faultline A boundary where two of the giant plates that form Earth's crust meet and grind against one another.

▼ *This highway in San Francisco, USA, collapsed during the earthquake of 1989.*

Immigrant A person who has arrived in a new country, having left their own.

Lahar A fast-moving flow caused by a volcano, usually containing ash and rocks mixed with melted snow or rain.

Lava Melted rock that flows from a volcano.

Mantle The red-hot layer of rock below Earth's outer crust, part of which is soft and behaves like a liquid.

Meteor A chunk of rock or dust from outer space that enters Earth's atmosphere and burns up to form a 'shooting star'.

Meteorite A chunk of rock from space that survives the trip through Earth's atmosphere to crash-land on Earth.

▲ A river of burning lava circles a hill in Hawaii during a volcanic eruption.

Plague A deadly disease that spreads rapidly or anything that causes suffering, such as a plague of locusts.

Tectonic plate One of the giant pieces that make up Earth's crust. The whole crust is made up of about a dozen of these plates.

Tsunami A giant wave which may be triggered by an earthquake or volcanic eruption. Tsunami are also called tidal waves, but they are not caused by tides.

Volcano An opening in Earth's crust through which lava, ash, rocks and steam from deep underground burst during an eruption.

DISASTER PROJECTS

Most earthquakes and eruptions occur in danger zones, where local experts keep a close eye on conditions. Find out more about these and other natural disasters by visiting museums and libraries or by logging on to earthquake, volcano and meteor sites on the Internet.

Most natural disasters don't strike just anywhere. Earthquakes and volcanic eruptions mainly happen along the edges of the huge plates that make up Earth's crust. These giant sections of crust are known as tectonic plates. They may carry a region of land, ocean or both.

The map shows Earth's tectonic plates. Trace the map or make a larger copy of it on a photocopier. Now use an atlas to find the locations of the earthquakes, eruptions and other natural disasters described in this book. Mark the places on the map. How many of the disasters happened along the edges of plates?

▶ *The yellow lines on this map show the borders between Earth's tectonic plates. Most volcanoes and earthquakes occur along these borders. This is because Earth's outer crust is weakest there.*

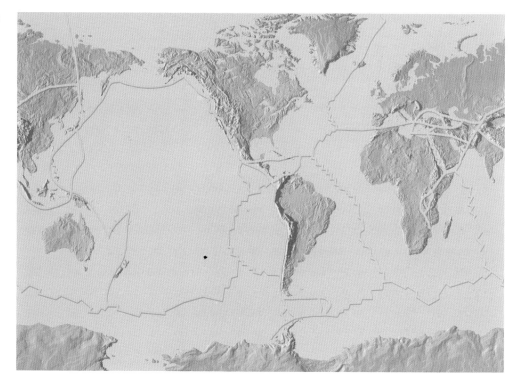

In parts of the world threatened by earthquakes and volcanoes, many schools run safety drills (like fire drills) which teach children what to do if disaster strikes. You could contact a school in one of these areas, either by post or via the Internet. San Francisco, USA, and Tokyo, Japan, are two examples of cities near dangerous regions. Find out about drills and other safety features that have been set up at the school.

▼ *Scientists take samples of gas in a volcano in Indonesia, in an effort to predict when the volcano will erupt.*

NATURAL DISASTER WEBSITES

If you have access to the Internet, there are hundreds of websites you can use to find out more about natural disasters.

Websites change from time to time, so don't worry if you can't find some of these sites. You can also search for sites featuring earthquakes, volcanoes and meteorites using any search engine.

GENERAL DISASTER WEBSITE:
Global Disaster Watch:
www.angelfire.com/on/predictions

EARTHQUAKE WEBSITES
Earthquake Information Network:
www.eqnet.org
Global Earthquake Response Center:
www.earthquake.com
Earthquake Research Institute, University of Tokyo:
www.eri.u-tokyo.ac.jp

VOLCANO WEBSITES
Weekly Volcano Activity Report:
www.volcano.si.edu/gvp/usgs
Volcano world:
http://volcano.und.nodak.edu

METEOR WATCH WEBSITES
Sky and Telescope's Meteor Page:
http://SkyandTelescope.com/observing/objects/meteors/
Space Weather and Meteor News:
www.spaceweather.com
Skywatch Meteor News:
www.sky-watch.com

INDEX